cont

British & North American Readers:
Please note that Australian cup and spoon measurements are metric. A quick conversion guide appears on page 63. A glossary explaining unfamiliar terms and ingredients begins on page 60.

vegetarian variety

If you've chosen a vegetarian diet, the most important point to remember is that variety is the key to good health. To obtain all of the necessary nutrients, you should eat from four main food groups every day: cereals and grains; pulses, nuts and seeds; fruit and vegetables; and soy and/or dairy products.

the four food groups

Some examples of **cereals and grains** include barley, buckwheat, maize, millet, oats, rye, wheat and rice. Vegetarian staples from this category are polenta, pasta, couscous, bread, noodles and, of course, rice.

The **pulses, nuts and seeds** category includes dried or canned beans and peas, in all of their varieties, lentils, nuts, such as cashews, pine nuts, macadamias, almonds, peanuts and walnuts, and seeds such as sunflower, sesame and pumpkin, to name a few.

The **fruit and vegetables** food group is self-explanatory, but it should be noted that dried fruit and vegetables are also included in the category. Finally, the **soy and/or dairy products** group includes milks, cheeses and yogurt, as well as tofu and tempeh.

supplementing your intake

A commonly held view is that a vegetarian diet, when eaten in conjunction with vitamin and mineral supplements, will be nutritionally sound. But a word of warning: vitamin and mineral supplements are recommended to treat deficiencies rather than as preventatives, as their long-term use can have unwanted side-effects. Some iron supplements can cause either diarrhoea or constipation, and large doses can interfere with the absorption of other minerals, such as zinc and copper. Similarly, large doses of zinc can reduce the absorption of copper and iron, while calcium supplements reduce iron and zinc absorption. Wherever possible, try to meet your nutrient needs via a balanced diet. The following tips might help eradicate the need for supplements.

zinc

If you eat seafood every now and again, you'll find that eating a plate of fresh oysters is the best dietary source of zinc. Good plant sources include pulses, nuts, seeds, and wholegrain breads and cereals – eat these foods daily. To aid absorption of zinc, eat some animal protein at the same time, for example, have yogurt or milk with wholegrain cereals, or have an egg on toast.

calcium

Dairy products (milk, cheese, yogurt) are the richest dietary source of calcium, but other good sources of calcium for vegetarians include calcium-enriched soy milk, leafy green vegetables (especially Asian greens and broccoli), figs, sesame seeds and tahini.

iron

Good sources of iron for vegetarians include breakfast cereals that have been fortified with iron, sunflower and sesame seeds, most types of nuts, peanut butter, chickpeas, soy beans and flour, lentils, tofu, red kidney beans and other beans (such as baked beans), wholemeal flour, wheat bran, wheatgerm and dried fruits (figs, raisins, apricots, peaches and prunes).

pad thai

600g fresh rice noodles

2¹/₂ tablespoons peanut oil

4 eggs, beaten lightly

300g tempeh, chopped finely

1 large brown onion (200g), sliced thinly

2 cloves garlic, crushed

2 tablespoons brown sugar

2 tablespoons sweet chilli sauce

2 tablespoons light soy sauce

1 tablespoon tomato sauce

2 cups (160g) bean sprouts

²/₃ cup (100g) unsalted roasted peanuts, chopped coarsely

1 tablespoon coarsely chopped fresh coriander

Rinse noodles under hot water; drain. Transfer to large bowl; separate noodles with fork.
Heat 1 teaspoon of the oil in wok; pour in half of the egg, swirl wok so egg forms a thin omelette; cook until set. Remove omelette from wok; repeat with remaining egg. Roll omelettes tightly; slice thinly.
Heat half of the remaining oil in wok; stir-fry tempeh until browned, remove from wok. Heat remaining oil in wok; stir-fry onion and garlic until onion is soft. Add noodles, sliced omelette, tempeh, sugar, sauces, sprouts and half of the nuts; stir-fry, tossing until heated through. Serve sprinkled with remaining nuts and coriander.

SERVES 4
Per serving 33.7g fat; 3225kJ

hokkien noodles

with cashews and vegetables

600g hokkien noodles

500g fresh firm tofu

1/2 cup (125ml) hoisin sauce

1/3 cup (80ml) light soy sauce

1 tablespoon peanut oil

1 cup (150g) raw cashews

6 green onions, chopped coarsely

2 cloves garlic, crushed

1 medium green capsicum (200g), sliced thinly

1 medium yellow capsicum (200g), sliced thinly

150g snow peas

150g baby spinach leaves

1/2 cup (125ml) vegetable stock

1 cup (80g) bean sprouts

Rinse noodles in hot water; drain. Transfer to large bowl; separate noodles with fork.
Cut tofu into 2cm cubes; combine with sauces in medium bowl.
Heat half of the oil in wok; stir-fry nuts until browned lightly, remove from wok.
Heat remaining oil in wok; stir-fry onion and garlic until onion is soft. Add capsicums and peas; stir-fry until vegetables are just tender. Add noodles, nuts, undrained tofu mixture, spinach, stock and sprouts; stir-fry, tossing gently until spinach is just wilted and noodles are heated through.

SERVES 4
Per serving 35.5g fat; 3793kJ

warm beetroot

and macadamia salad

8 medium
beetroot (1.4kg)

40g ghee

2 small leeks
(400g), sliced thinly

1 cup (150g)
macadamias

1/4 cup (60ml)
raspberry vinegar

1/4 cup (60ml)
olive oil

1 clove garlic,
crushed

250g baby
rocket leaves

250g baby
spinach leaves

150g goat cheese,
crumbled

Boil, steam or microwave beetroot until tender;
drain. Peel beetroot while warm; cut into wedges.
Heat ghee in wok; stir-fry leek and nuts until leek
is soft and nuts are browned lightly.
Add beetroot, vinegar, oil and garlic to wok;
stir-fry, tossing until beetroot is heated through.
Toss rocket, spinach and cheese through
beetroot mixture off the heat.

SERVES 4
Per serving 59.3g fat; 3032kJ

8 pumpkin and
white-bean curry

1kg piece pumpkin

2 tablespoons peanut oil

1 medium brown onion (150g)

2 cloves garlic, crushed

1 teaspoon grated fresh ginger

$1/2$ teaspoon caraway seeds

300g asparagus, chopped coarsely

2 tablespoons korma curry paste

300g can white beans, rinsed, drained

$2/3$ cup (160ml) coconut milk

50g baby spinach leaves, halved

1 tablespoon finely shredded fresh basil

Preheat oven to very hot. Cut pumpkin into
3cm pieces, toss with half of the oil in large baking
dish; bake, uncovered, in very hot oven about
15 minutes or until browned and tender.

Cut onion into thin wedges. Heat remaining oil in
wok; stir-fry onion, garlic, ginger and seeds until
onion is soft. Add asparagus and paste; stir-fry
2 minutes. Add pumpkin, beans, milk, spinach and
basil; stir-fry, tossing gently until heated through.

SERVES 4
Per serving 22.1g fat; 1307kJ

grated vegetables with
chilli and angel-hair pasta

500g angel hair pasta

90g butter

¼ cup (60ml) olive oil

1 medium red onion (170g), chopped finely

2 cloves garlic, crushed

1 red thai chilli, chopped finely

2 medium green zucchini (240g), grated coarsely

2 medium carrots (240g), grated coarsely

1 medium kumara (400g), grated coarsely

1 tablespoon finely chopped fresh oregano

1 cup (80g) finely grated parmsean cheese

Cook pasta in large saucepan of boiling water, uncovered, until just tender; drain.
Heat butter and oil in wok; stir-fry onion, garlic, chilli and vegetables about 10 minutes or until vegetables are browned lightly and tender.
Add pasta to wok with oregano and half of the cheese; stir-fry, tossing until heated through.
Serve topped with remaining cheese.

SERVES 6
Per serving 26.9g fat; 2455kJ

pepper-cream
vegetables

1 tablespoon olive oil

2 medium brown
onions (300g),
sliced thinly

2 medium carrots
(240g), sliced thinly

4 baby eggplants
(240g), sliced thinly

1 clove garlic, crushed

250g button
mushrooms, halved

2 medium green
zucchini (240g),
sliced thinly

1 medium red
capsicum (200g),
sliced thinly

1/2 cup (125ml)
vegetable stock

1/2 cup (125ml) cream

2 tablespoons cracked
black pepper

Heat oil in wok; stir-fry all vegetables, in batches, until just tender.
Add stock, cream and pepper to same wok; stir until sauce
thickens slightly.
Serve vegetables with sauce.

SERVES 4
Per serving 19.1g fat; 1076kJ

crisp green vegetables
with tempeh

2 tablespoons
peanut oil

300g tempeh,
chopped finely

1 medium brown onion
(150g), sliced thinly

3 cloves garlic,
crushed

500g asparagus,
halved lengthways

200g sugar snap peas

200g baby
bok choy, halved

200g bean sprouts

1/4 cup (60ml)
light soy sauce

1/4 cup (60ml) mirin

2 tablespoons
rice vinegar

Heat half of the oil in wok; stir-fry tempeh until
browned, remove from wok.
Heat remaining oil in wok; stir-fry onion and
garlic until onion is soft. Add asparagus to wok;
stir-fry until tender. Add peas and bok choy;
stir-fry, tossing until bok choy is just wilted.
Add remaining ingredients; stir-fry until sauce
comes to a boil. Toss tempeh with vegetables.

SERVES 4
Per serving 13.3g fat; 1127kJ

spicy combination
fried rice

You will need about 2 cups (400g) uncooked long-grain rice for this recipe.

2¹/₂ tablespoons peanut oil

4 eggs, beaten lightly

1 medium brown onion (150g), chopped finely

2 cloves garlic, crushed

1 teaspoon grated fresh ginger

1 red thai chilli, seeded, chopped finely

1 cup (80g) shredded chinese cabbage

130g can corn kernels, drained

¹/₂ cup (60g) frozen peas

6 cups cooked white rice

2 tablespoons light soy sauce

1 tablespoon kecap manis

220g packet fried tofu, chopped coarsely

2 cups (160g) bean sprouts

1 teaspoon sesame oil

Heat 2 teaspoons of the peanut oil in wok; pour in half of the egg, swirl wok so egg forms a thin omelette; cook until set. Remove omelette from wok; repeat with remaining egg. Roll omelettes tightly; cut into thin slices.
Heat remaining peanut oil in wok; stir-fry onion, garlic, ginger and chilli until onion is soft. Add cabbage, corn and peas; stir-fry 2 minutes.
Add rice, sauces, tofu, sprouts, sesame oil and sliced omelette; stir-fry, tossing until hot.

SERVES 4
Per serving 25g fat; 2899kJ

cantonese spinach
and almonds

2 teaspoons peanut oil

1/3 cup (25g)
flaked almonds

2 tablespoons
sweet sherry

2 tablespoons
light soy sauce

2 tablespoons honey

1 clove garlic, crushed

1/2 teaspoon
sesame oil

1kg spinach, trimmed

6 green onions,
chopped finely

Heat peanut oil in wok; stir-fry nuts until just browned, remove
from wok. Cook sherry, soy sauce, honey, garlic and sesame oil
in same wok until sauce boils.
Add spinach and onion; stir-fry, tossing until spinach is just wilted.
Serve spinach mixture with nuts sprinkled over the top.

SERVES 4
Per serving 6.8g fat; 626kJ

chilli beans
with tofu

2 tablespoons
vegetable oil

375g fresh firm tofu,
chopped coarsely

1 medium brown onion
(150g), sliced thinly

1 medium green
capsicum (200g),
chopped finely

425g can kidney
beans, rinsed, drained

400g can tomatoes,
drained, crushed

1 tablespoon
hot chilli sauce

1/4 cup (70g)
tomato paste

2 tablespoons
tomato sauce

1/2 cup (125ml) water

Heat half of the oil in wok; stir-fry tofu,
in batches, until browned, drain on
absorbent paper.
Heat remaining oil in same wok; stir-fry onion
and capsicum, tossing until onion is soft.
Return tofu to wok with remaining ingredients;
stir-fry, tossing gently until heated through.

SERVES 4
Per serving 16.4g fat; 1290kJ

chilli lime

green-bean trio

1 tablespoon olive oil

250g snake beans,
chopped coarsely

350g frozen broad
beans, thawed, peeled

350g green beans

chilli lime dressing

1 tablespoon olive oil

2 teaspoons finely
grated lime rind

2 tablespoons
lime juice

$1/2$ teaspoon
sambal oelek

1 teaspoon finely
chopped fresh mint

1 tablespoon finely
chopped fresh basil

1 clove garlic, crushed

Heat oil in wok; stir-fry all beans, in batches, until tender. Return
beans to wok with half of the chilli lime dressing; stir until hot.
Just before serving, combine bean mixture with remaining chilli
lime dressing in large bowl.
Chilli Lime Dressing Combine ingredients in jar; shake well.

SERVES 4
Per serving 9.7g fat; 633kJ

potatoes and
kumara with fetta

1kg tiny new potatoes, halved

1 medium kumara (400g), chopped coarsely

1 tablespoon olive oil

30g butter

1 large red onion (300g), sliced thinly

½ cup (80g) pine nuts

1 tablespoon finely chopped fresh rosemary

1 tablespoon seeded mustard

200g fetta, chopped finely

1 tablespoon finely chopped fresh chives

Boil, steam or microwave potato and kumara until just tender; drain.

Heat oil and butter in wok; stir-fry potato and kumara, in batches, until browned and tender.

Add onion and nuts to wok; stir-fry until onion is soft and nuts are browned.

Return potato and kumara to wok with rosemary and mustard; stir-fry, tossing until heated through.

Remove wok from heat; toss through cheese, sprinkle with chives.

SERVES 4
Per serving 36.9g fat; 2583kJ

satay noodle

combination

2 tablespoons peanut oil

375g fresh firm tofu, chopped coarsely

500g hokkien noodles

1 medium brown onion (150g), chopped finely

1 clove garlic, crushed

1 teaspoon grated fresh ginger

1 teaspoon mild curry powder

100g green beans, halved

100g snow peas, halved

1/2 cup (140g) crunchy peanut butter

1/4 cup (60ml) sweet chilli sauce

1 tablespoon lime juice

1 cup (250ml) coconut milk

3/4 cup (180ml) vegetable stock

1 cup (80g) bean sprouts

1 tablespoon finely chopped fresh coriander

Heat 1 tablespoon of the oil in wok; stir-fry tofu, in batches, until browned, drain on absorbent paper.
Rinse noodles under hot water; drain. Transfer to large bowl; separate noodles with a fork.
Heat remaining oil in same wok; stir-fry onion, garlic and ginger until onion is soft. Add curry powder; stir-fry until fragrant. Add beans and peas; stir-fry 1 minute.
Add noodles and combined peanut butter, sauce, juice, milk and stock; stir-fry, tossing until noodles are heated through and sauce comes to a boil. Add tofu, sprouts and coriander; stir-fry, tossing gently until hot.

SERVES 4
Per serving 48.3g fat; 3767kJ

kumara and broccoli
with cumin yogurt dressing

3 medium kumara
(1.2kg), sliced thickly

160g broccoli florets

1 tablespoon
peanut oil

2 large brown onions
(400g), sliced thinly

2 cloves garlic,
crushed

2 teaspoons
sambal oelek

**cumin yogurt
dressing**

1/2 cup (140g) yogurt

1/2 teaspoon
ground coriander

1 teaspoon
ground cumin

1 tablespoon water

2 tablespoons
lemon juice

Boil, steam or microwave kumara and broccoli,
separately, until almost tender; drain.
Meanwhile, heat oil in wok; stir-fry onion, garlic
and sambal until onion is browned lightly.
Add kumara and broccoli; stir-fry, tossing
until vegetables are heated through. Just before
serving, drizzle with cumin yogurt dressing.
Cumin Yogurt Dressing Combine ingredients
in small bowl.

SERVES 4
Per serving 6.4g fat; 1183kJ

masala okra

2 tablespoons ghee

2 medium brown onions (300g), sliced thinly

2 teaspoons grated fresh ginger

2 cloves garlic, crushed

1 teaspoon black mustard seeds

1 red thai chilli, sliced thinly

1 teaspoon garam masala

2 teaspoons ground cumin

500g okra

1 cup (250ml) water

1/2 cup (125ml) coconut milk

1 tablespoon finely chopped fresh coriander

Heat ghee in wok; stir-fry onion, ginger and garlic until onion is soft. Add seeds, chilli and spices; stir-fry until fragrant.
Add okra and the water; cook, uncovered, about 30 minutes or until okra is soft and liquid has evaporated. Add coconut milk and coriander; stir until heated through.

SERVES 4
Per serving 15.7g fat; 823kJ

vietnamese-style fried tofu

220g packet fried tofu

1/3 cup (80ml) light soy sauce

2 tablespoons finely chopped
fresh coriander

1 teaspoon honey

6 dried shiitake mushrooms

2 medium carrots (240g)

200g snake beans

1 tablespoon peanut oil

3 cloves garlic, crushed

1 1/2 teaspoons grated
fresh ginger

1 tablespoon finely chopped
fresh lemon grass

1/2 small cauliflower (500g),
chopped coarsely

230g can bamboo shoots,
rinsed, drained

1 medium chinese cabbage
(600g), chopped coarsely

1 tablespoon cornflour

3/4 cup (180ml)
vegetable stock

2 teaspoons hoisin sauce

1 teaspoon lime juice

1/2 teaspoon sambal oelek

Cut tofu into 1cm thick slices. Combine tofu in medium bowl with soy, coriander and honey.
Place mushrooms in small heatproof bowl, cover with boiling water; stand 20 minutes. Drain mushrooms, discard stems; slice caps thinly.
Cut carrots into thin 6cm strips. Cut beans into 6cm lengths. Heat oil in wok; stir-fry garlic, ginger and lemon grass until fragrant. Add carrot, beans and cauliflower; stir-fry until vegetables are just tender.
Add tofu mixture to wok with bamboo shoots, mushrooms and cabbage; stir-fry, tossing until heated through.
Stir in blended cornflour and stock, sauce, juice and sambal; stir over heat until sauce boils and thickens slightly.

SERVES 4
Per serving 11.9g fat; 965kJ

asian-style vegetables
with mushrooms

8 dried shiitake
mushrooms

1 tablespoon
peanut oil

2 cloves garlic,
crushed

2 teaspoons grated
fresh ginger

100g black fungi

150g shimeji
mushrooms

425g can straw
mushrooms, drained

200g broccoli florets

500g choy sum,
chopped coarsely

300g baby bok choy,
chopped coarsely

1/4 cup (60ml)
light soy sauce

2 tablespoons sweet
chilli sauce

1 tablespoon
hoisin sauce

1 tablespoon
rice vinegar

Place dried mushrooms in small heatproof
bowl, cover with boiling water; stand
20 minutes. Drain mushrooms, discard
stems; slice caps thinly.
Heat oil in wok; stir-fry garlic, ginger and all
mushrooms for 1 minute. Add broccoli, choy
sum and bok choy; stir-fry 2 minutes.
Add combined sauces and vinegar; stir-fry,
tossing until choy sum and bok choy are just
wilted and sauce comes to a boil.

SERVES 4
Per serving 6.1g fat; 536kJ

*1½ cups (300g)
red lentils*

¼ cup (60ml) olive oil

*2 green onions,
chopped finely*

1 clove garlic, crushed

*1 medium carrot
(120g), chopped finely*

*1 medium red
capsicum (200g),
chopped finely*

*2 medium green
zucchini (240g),
chopped finely*

*1 trimmed celery stick
(75g), chopped finely*

*2 large egg tomatoes
(180g), seeded,
chopped finely*

*2 tablespoons red
wine vinegar*

1 teaspoon sugar

*1 tablespoon finely
chopped fresh mint*

*1 tablespoon finely
chopped fresh
flat-leaf parsley*

Cook lentils in large saucepan of boiling
water, uncovered, about 8 minutes or until
just tender, drain.

Heat oil in wok; stir-fry onion, garlic, carrot,
capsicum, zucchini and celery, tossing until
vegetables are just tender. Remove wok from
heat, add lentils and remaining ingredients;
toss until combined.

SERVES 4
Per serving 15.5g fat; 1483kJ

singapore noodles

8 dried shiitake mushrooms

2 tablespoons peanut oil

200g tempeh, chopped finely

3 cloves garlic, crushed

1 tablespoon grated
fresh ginger

2 tablespoons mild
curry paste

600g fresh singapore noodles

230g can water chestnuts,
drained, chopped coarsely

425g can baby corn, drained,
chopped coarsely

4 green onions,
chopped finely

2 tablespoons
light soy sauce

2 tablespoons kecap manis

2 tablespoons
vegetable stock

3 eggs, beaten lightly

2 teaspoons sesame oil

Place mushrooms in small heatproof bowl, cover with boiling water; stand 20 minutes. Drain mushrooms, discard stems; slice caps thinly.

Heat peanut oil in wok; stir-fry tempeh until browned lightly, remove from wok. Add garlic, ginger and paste to wok; stir-fry until fragrant.

Rinse noodles under cold water; drain.

Add mushrooms, noodles, tempeh, water chestnuts, corn, onion, sauces and stock to wok; stir-fry, tossing until hot.

Add combined eggs and sesame oil; stir-fry, tossing until eggs are just cooked.

SERVES 4
Per serving 24.2g fat; 3109kJ

wild rice with snow peas
and baby beets

¹/₃ cup (60g) wild rice

¹/₃ cup (65g) basmati rice

1 tablespoon olive oil

6 spring onions, halved

1 clove garlic, crushed

4 medium yellow zucchini (480g), sliced thinly

150g snow peas, halved

1 cup (100g) mung bean sprouts

10 canned baby beets, drained, halved

Cook wild rice in large saucepan of boiling water, uncovered, about 20 minutes or until tender, drain.
Cook basmati rice in large saucepan of boiling water, uncovered, about 12 minutes or until just tender; drain.
Heat oil in wok; stir-fry onion, garlic and zucchini until zucchini is just tender. Add snow peas, rices and sprouts; stir-fry, tossing until hot. Stir in beets just before serving.

SERVES 4
Per serving 5.4g fat; 896kJ

lentil balls with
tomatoes and rocket

1 cup (200g) red lentils

2 tablespoons olive oil

2 medium green zucchini (240g), grated coarsely

1 small brown onion (80g), chopped finely

1 red thai chilli, chopped finely

1 cup (70g) stale breadcrumbs

1/4 cup (35g) sesame seeds, toasted

1 tablespoon finely chopped fresh coriander

1/3 cup (35g) packaged breadcrumbs

vegetable oil, for deep-frying

5 medium egg tomatoes (375g), quartered

2 cloves garlic, crushed

120g rocket, trimmed

2 tablespoons finely shredded fresh mint

2 tablespoons finely shredded fresh basil

2 tablespoons white wine vinegar

Cook lentils in large saucepan of boiling water, uncovered, 8 minutes or until tender; drain.
Heat half of the olive oil in wok; stir-fry zucchini, onion and chilli until onion is soft. Combine lentils, zucchini mixture, stale breadcrumbs, seeds and coriander in large bowl; roll rounded teaspoons of mixture into balls, toss in packaged breadcrumbs.
Heat vegetable oil in large saucepan; deep-fry lentil balls, in batches, until browned; drain.
Heat remaining olive oil in same wok; stir-fry remaining ingredients, tossing until rocket is just wilted. Add lentil balls; stir until hot.

SERVES 4
Per serving 25.7g fat; 1987kJ

spiced eggplant

2 cups (400g) couscous

2 cups (500ml) boiling water

2¹/₂ tablespoons olive oil

¹/₃ cup (50g) pine nuts

2 medium eggplants (600g), chopped coarsely

2 teaspoons ground cumin

2 teaspoons ground coriander

300g can chickpeas, rinsed, drained

1 cup (230g) fresh dates, seeded, chopped coarsely

2 tablespoons fresh coriander leaves

2 tablespoons fresh flat-leaf parsley

2 tablespoons fresh mint leaves

honey dressing

2 tablespoons olive oil

2 teaspoons finely grated lemon rind

2 tablespoons lemon juice

2 tablespoons honey

¹/₂ teaspoon ground cinnamon

Combine couscous and the water in large heatproof bowl, cover; stand 5 minutes or until liquid is absorbed, fluffing with fork occasionally
Heat 2 teaspoons of the oil in wok; stir-fry nuts until browned lightly, remove from wok.
Combine half of the remaining oil with eggplant, cumin and ground coriander in large bowl.
Heat remaining oil in wok; stir-fry eggplant mixture, in batches, until browned and tender. Return eggplant to wok with couscous, remaining ingredients and honey dressing; stir-fry, tossing until heated through.
Honey Dressing Combine ingredients in jar; shake well.

SERVES 4
Per serving 31.7g fat; 3410kJ

peas, beans and leaves

We've all done it... that is, mistake one green for another or a leafy bunch for something completely different. This pictorial guide will help you pick the vegetable variety first time, every time.

peas and beans

Green beans, sometimes called french beans, are thin, round bean pods. They are eaten whole, having been "topped and tailed", and are suitable for use raw or cooked.

Butter beans, also known as wax or yellow beans, are thin, round, bean pods that are creamy-yellow in colour. They can be eaten raw or cooked.

Snake beans are long (about 40cm), thin, round, dark-green beans which are Asian in origin; they are sold in bunches.

Snow peas, also known as mange tout, sugar peas or chinese peas, are flat pods containing barely formed peas. They, are eaten whole, not podded, and are tasty raw or cooked.

Broad beans, also known as fava beans, are available fresh in a long, green outer pod. They're best when peeled twice – first, the outer pod should be removed, then the sandy-green inner shell – to reveal the bright-green broad bean.

Sugar snap peas are small pods that contain tiny, formed peas. They are eaten whole, not podded, and are delicious raw or cooked.

leaves

Baby bok choy, also known as pak choi or chinese white cabbage, has a mild cabbage flavour and the leaves and stems are used, either raw or cooked.

Choy sum, also known as flowering boy choy or flowering white cabbage, is a popular Chinese green that can often be seen sporting yellow flowers. Both the flowering stems and the leaves are eaten.

Chinese cabbage, also known as peking cabbage or wong bok, is a large pale-green cabbage with thick white stems. It is best used as a salad vegetable, or cooked for only a very short time.

Spinach, often mistakenly called silverbeet, is a thin-stemmed vegetable with delicate, green leaves. It can be eaten raw or cooked.

Rocket, also known as arugula, rugula or rucola, has segmented green leaves with a delightful peppery flavour. Rocket is an ideal salad vegetable as well as being delicious when cooked.

Baby spinach leaves are a popular inclusion in salads, and can be eaten raw or cooked.

Baby rocket, a smaller version of rocket (see above), is particularly well suited to use in salads.

ravioli with semi-dried
tomatoes

500g spinach and
ricotta ravioli

2 tablespoons olive oil

1/2 cup (80g) pine nuts

1 medium red onion
(170g), chopped finely

2 cloves garlic, crushed

2 medium green zucchini
(240g), sliced thinly

2 baby eggplants (120g),
sliced thinly

1/2 cup (125ml) cream

100g baby spinach leaves

1/2 cup (75g) drained
semi-dried tomatoes,
chopped coarsely

2 teaspoons finely
chopped fresh thyme

1 cup (80g) flaked
parmesan cheese

Cook pasta in large saucepan of boiling water, uncovered, until just tender; drain.

Heat 1 teaspoon of the oil in wok; stir-fry nuts until browned, remove from wok.

Heat remaining oil in wok; stir-fry onion, garlic, zucchini and eggplant, tossing until vegetables are tender.

Add pasta, cream, spinach, tomato and thyme; stir-fry, tossing until heated through. Serve topped with cheese.

SERVES 4
Per serving 51.3g fat; 2828kJ

warm vegetable salad with
macadamias

150g green beans

2 tablespoons olive oil

250g broccoli florets

150g sugar snap peas

150g snow peas

250g cherry tomatoes

60g snow pea sprouts

4 green onions,
chopped finely

1 cup (150g)
macadamias, chopped
coarsely, toasted

dressing

1/3 cup (80ml) extra
virgin olive oil

1/4 cup (60ml) red
wine vinegar

1 tablespoon finely
chopped fresh thyme

1 teaspoon sugar

1 teaspoon cracked
black pepper

Cut beans into 5cm lengths. Heat oil in wok;
stir-fry beans, broccoli and peas for 1 minute.
Add tomatoes, sprouts, onion, half of the nuts
and dressing; stir-fry, tossing until heated
through. Serve sprinkled with remaining nuts.
Dressing Combine ingredients in jar; shake well.

SERVES 4
Per serving 56.7g fat; 2578kJ

saffron couscous with
raisins and almonds

1 cup (250ml) vegetable stock

1/2 cup (125ml) water

1 1/2 cups (300g) couscous

2 tablespoons olive oil

4 small brown onions (320g), quartered

2 cloves garlic, crushed

1/4 teaspoon saffron powder

1/2 teaspoon garam masala

1 teaspoon sweet paprika

1/2 cup (85g) raisins

1 medium yellow zucchini (120g), sliced thinly

1 medium carrot (120g), sliced thinly

1/4 cup (60ml) sherry vinegar

300g can chickpeas, drained

1/3 cup (55g) almond kernels, toasted, chopped coarsely

Bring stock and the water to a boil in medium saucepan; stir in coucsous. Remove from heat, cover; stand 5 minutes or until liquid is absorbed, fluffing with fork occasionally.
Heat oil in wok; stir-fry onion until browned lightly. Add garlic and spices; stir-fry until fragrant. Add raisins, zucchini and carrot; stir-fry until vegetables are just tender. Add vinegar, chickpeas, couscous and nuts; stir-fry, tossing until just heated through.

SERVES 4
Per serving 18.9g fat; 2491kJ

eggplant and
salsa fresca

10 baby eggplants (600g)

2 tablespoons peanut oil

1 medium white onion
(150g), sliced thinly

2 cloves garlic, crushed

1 teaspoon sambal oelek

1 cup (250ml)
tomato juice

6 green onions,
chopped finely

salsa fresca

1 lebanese
cucumber (130g)

1 large tomato (250g),
seeded, chopped finely

1 trimmed stick celery
(75g), chopped finely

1/4 teaspoon
Tabasco sauce

1 tablespoon lime juice

Halve eggplants lengthways; cut four long strips through each piece lengthways, stopping about 1cm from stem end.

Heat half of the oil in wok; stir-fry eggplant, in batches, until just browned.

Heat remaining oil in same wok; stir-fry white onion, garlic and sambal until fragrant. Return eggplant to wok with juice; stir-fry until eggplant is tender.

Serve eggplant mixture topped with salsa fresca and green onion.

Salsa Fresca Halve cucumber lengthways; remove and discard seeds, chop flesh in small dice. Combine cucumber in small bowl with remaining ingredients.

SERVES 4
Per serving 9.8g fat; 648kJ

almond coriander

couscous

3 cups (600g) couscous

3 cups (750ml) boiling water

¼ cup (60ml) olive oil

¾ cup (105g) slivered almonds

1 clove garlic, crushed

2 green onions, chopped finely

⅓ cup (50g) dried currants

*½ cup finely chopped
fresh coriander*

Combine couscous and the water in large heatproof bowl, cover; stand 5 minutes or until liquid is absorbed, fluffing with fork occasionally.

Heat 2 teaspoons of the oil in wok; stir-fry nuts until browned lightly, remove from wok. Heat remaining oil in same wok; stir-fry garlic and onion until onion is soft.

Add couscous to wok; stir-fry, tossing until heated through. Stir in nuts, currants and coriander.

SERVES 4
Per serving 29.2g fat; 3615kJ

marinated tofu
on crisp noodles

9 dried shiitake
mushrooms

500g fresh
firm tofu

1/4 cup (60ml)
hoisin sauce

2 tablespoons
tomato sauce

1/4 cup finely chopped
fresh lemon grass

3 red thai chillies,
chopped finely

1 large brown onion
(200g), chopped finely

4 cloves garlic,
crushed

1/4 cup finely chopped
fresh coriander

vegetable oil,
for deep-frying

100g thin rice
stick noodles

2 teaspoons peanut oil

1 medium red
capsicum (200g),
sliced thinly

100g snow peas,
halved

Place mushrooms in small heatproof bowl,
cover with boiling water; stand 20 minutes. Drain
mushrooms, discard stems; slice caps thinly.
Meanwhile, cut tofu into 3cm pieces. Combine
sauces, lemon grass, chilli, onion, garlic,
coriander and tofu in medium bowl. Cover;
stand 20 minutes.
Heat vegetable oil in wok; deep-fry noodles in
hot oil until puffed, drain on absorbent paper.
Remove tofu from marinade; reserve marinade.
Heat peanut oil in clean wok; stir-fry tofu, in
batches, until browned lightly.
Add capsicum, snow peas, mushrooms and
reserved marinade to wok; stir-fry 3 minutes.
Add tofu; stir-fry, tossing until heated through.
Serve tofu mixture on noodles.

SERVES 4
Per serving 14.6g fat; 1437kJ

indian-style
vegetables

1 tablespoon
peanut oil

1 clove garlic, crushed

1 teaspoon
ground cumin

1 teaspoon
ground caraway

1 teaspoon
ground nutmeg

1 teaspoon mild
curry powder

1/2 teaspoon
ground turmeric

1 medium brown onion
(150g), sliced thinly

1 medium carrot
(120g), sliced thinly

300g yellow squash,
quartered

1 medium green
capsicum (200g),
sliced thinly

200g button
mushrooms, halved

1 teaspoon cornflour

3/4 cup (180ml)
coconut cream

1 tablespoon finely
chopped fresh
coriander

Heat oil in wok; stir-fry garlic and spices until fragrant. Add onion and carrot; stir-fry until onion is soft. Add squash, capsicum and mushrooms; stir-fry 2 minutes.
Add blended cornflour and coconut cream; stir-fry, tossing until sauce boils and thickens slightly. Serve sprinkled with coriander.

SERVES 4
Per serving 14.7g fat; 842kJ

sugar snap and snow peas
with tofu and pistachios

2 tablespoons
peanut oil

600g fresh firm tofu,
chopped coarsely

1 cup (150g)
shelled pistachios

30g butter

2 cloves garlic,
crushed

2 red thai chillies,
seeded, chopped finely

2 teaspoons grated
fresh ginger

400g sugar snap peas

400g snow peas

1/4 cup (60ml) sweet
chilli sauce

Heat half of the oil in wok; stir-fry tofu and nuts,
in batches, until tofu is browned lightly.
Heat remaining oil, with butter, in same wok;
stir-fry garlic, chilli and ginger until fragrant.
Add peas to wok; stir-fry until just tender.
Return tofu and nuts to wok with sauce;
stir-fry, tossing to combine ingredients.

SERVES 4
Per serving 45.3g fat; 2552kJ

rice noodles with
omelette strips
and choy sum

600g fresh rice noodles

4 eggs

1 tablespoon water

2 tablespoons peanut oil

2 cloves garlic, crushed

2 teaspoons grated
fresh ginger

300g choy sum,
chopped coarsely

4 green onions,
chopped finely

2 tablespoons
light soy sauce

1 tablespoon sweet
chilli sauce

1 tablespoon hoisin sauce

1/2 cup (75g) unsalted
roasted peanuts

Rinse noodles under hot water; drain. Transfer to large bowl; separate noodles with fork.

Whisk eggs and the water in small bowl. Heat 2 teaspoons of the oil in wok; pour in half of the egg mixture, swirl wok so egg forms a thin omelette; cook until set. Remove omelette from wok; repeat with remaining egg mixture. Roll omelettes tightly; cut into thin slices.

Heat remaining oil in wok; stir-fry garlic, ginger, choy sum and onion until choy sum is just wilted. Add noodles, sauces, omelette strips and nuts; stir-fry, tossing until heated through.

SERVES 4
Per serving 25.1g fat; 2403kJ

nutty tabbouleh
salad

2 cups (320g) burghul

2 cloves garlic, crushed

1 cup tightly packed fresh basil leaves

2 teaspoons sugar

1/3 cup (80ml) olive oil

1/4 cup (60ml) lemon juice

1 tablespoon olive oil, extra

500g asparagus, chopped coarsely

2 lebanese cucumbers (260g), chopped coarsely

500g cherry tomatoes, halved

1/2 cup (50g) pecans, toasted

1/2 cup (80g) almond kernels, toasted

1/3 cup (50g) pine nuts, toasted

1/2 cup finely chopped fresh chives

200g cheddar cheese

1/2 cup finely chopped fresh flat-leaf parsley

Place burghul in medium heatproof bowl, cover with boiling water; stand 10 minutes. Drain burghul, rinse under cold water, drain; pat dry on absorbent paper.

Process garlic, basil and sugar until basil is finely chopped, add oil and juice; process until combined.

Heat extra oil in wok; stir-fry asparagus, cucumber and tomato until asparagus is just tender. Add burghul, basil mixture, most of the combined nuts and most of the chives; stir-fry, tossing until hot.

Cut cheese into thin strips; add to salad with parsley; top with remaining nuts and chives.

SERVES 4
Per serving 70.2g fat; 4129kJ

spicy **potato** and coriander salad

1kg tiny new potatoes, halved

1½ tablespoons olive oil

1 medium red onion (170g), chopped finely

3 cloves garlic, crushed

3 teaspoons ground cumin

1½ teaspoons ground coriander

1 teaspoon sweet paprika

½ teaspoon ground turmeric

¼ teaspoon ground cinnamon

½ cup finely chopped fresh coriander

dressing

⅓ cup (80ml) lemon juice

¼ cup (60ml) olive oil

½ teaspoon sambal oelek

1 teaspoon sugar

¼ teaspoon cracked black pepper

Boil, steam or microwave potatoes until just tender; drain.

Heat oil in wok; stir-fry onion, garlic and ground spices until onion is soft. Add potato and fresh coriander; stir-fry, tossing about 5 minutes or until potatoes are well coated and heated through.

Remove wok from heat, add dressing; toss gently.

Dressing Combine ingredients in jar; shake well.

SERVES 4
Per serving 21.3g fat; 1583kJ

rice **noodles**

with asian greens

250g fresh firm tofu

*250g fresh
rice noodles*

*1 tablespoon
peanut oil*

*1 large brown onion
(200g), sliced thickly*

*2 cloves garlic,
crushed*

*1 teaspoon
five-spice powder*

*300g button
mushrooms, halved*

*200g swiss brown
mushrooms, halved*

*¼ cup (60ml)
light soy sauce*

*1 cup (250ml)
vegetable stock*

¼ cup (60ml) water

*300g baby bok choy,
chopped coarsely*

*300g choy sum,
chopped coarsely*

*4 green onions,
chopped coarsely*

200g bean sprouts

Cut tofu into 2cm cubes. Rinse noodles under hot water; drain. Transfer to large bowl; separate noodles with fork.
Heat oil in wok; stir-fry brown onion and garlic until onion is soft. Add five-spice; stir-fry until fragrant. Add mushrooms; stir-fry until almost tender.
Add sauce, stock and the water; bring to a boil. Add bok choy, choy sum and green onion; stir-fry until bok choy just wilts. Add tofu, noodles and sprouts; stir-fry until hot.

SERVES 4
Per serving 9.3g fat; 1321kJ

beetroot-tinted noodles
with white beans

2 medium raw
beetroot (350g),
grated coarsely

350g dried
wheat noodles

2 tablespoons
vegetable oil

425g can white beans,
rinsed, drained

5 cloves garlic,
crushed

2 tablespoons
coarsely grated
lemon rind

12 fresh (or canned)
water chestnuts,
chopped coarsely

1/2 cup (125ml)
olive oil

1/4 cup (60ml)
balsamic vinegar

1/4 cup (60ml)
lemon juice

2 tablespoons finely
chopped fresh chives

2 teaspoons sugar

Bring 1.5 litres (6 cups) water to a boil in
large saucepan; simmer beetroot, uncovered,
5 minutes. Add noodles to pan; return to boil
then remove from heat immediately. Stand,
stirring occasionally, until noodles are just
tender and have absorbed beetroot colour.
Drain; cover to keep warm.

Heat vegetable oil in wok; stir-fry beans,
garlic, rind and water chestnuts until water
chestnuts are just tender and browned lightly.
Stir in combined remaining ingredients; stir-fry,
tossing until heated through.

Divide noodles among serving plates;
top with water chestnut mixture.

SERVES 4
Per serving 39.2g fat; 2940kJ

thai-style green
curry with
vegetables

2 medium
carrots (240g)

1 medium green
capsicum (200g)

250g broccoli florets

400ml can
coconut milk

375g fresh firm tofu,
chopped coarsely

curry paste

2 x 12cm fresh green
chillies, seeded,
chopped coarsely

3 green onions,
chopped coarsely

1/4 cup fresh
coriander leaves

2 tablespoons finely
chopped fresh
lemon grass

2 cloves garlic,
chopped coarsely

2 tablespoons
peanut oil

2 tablespoons water

1/2 teaspoon
ground cumin

Cut carrot and capsicum into thin strips.

Add curry paste to heated wok with carrot and capsicum; stir-fry 2 minutes. Add broccoli and coconut milk; stir-fry until sauce thickens slightly and broccoli is just tender. Add tofu; cook until hot.

Paste Blend or process ingredients until almost smooth.

SERVES 4
Per serving
36.6g fat; 1816kJ

snow peas and almonds
with egg noodles

500g hokkien noodles

1 tablespoon peanut oil

1 clove garlic, crushed

1 medium brown onion
(150g), sliced thinly

200g snow peas

2 tablespoons plum sauce

2 teaspoons light soy sauce

1/2 teaspoon cornflour

1/2 teaspoon sugar

1/2 cup (125ml)
vegetable stock

1/2 cup (80g) blanched
almonds, toasted

Rinse noodles under hot water;
drain. Transfer noodles to large bowl;
separate with fork.
Heat oil in wok; stir-fry garlic and onion
until soft. Add snow peas, noodles,
sauces and blended cornflour, sugar
and stock; stir-fry until sauce boils and
thickens slightly. Stir in nuts.

SERVES 4
Per serving 17.3g fat; 2258kJ

rosemary risoni with

italian-style vegetables

1 large red capsicum (350g)

1 large yellow capsicum (350g)

500g risoni pasta

400g can tomatoes

1/4 cup (70g) tomato paste

1 teaspoon sambal oelek

1 tablespoon olive oil

2 medium brown onions (300g), chopped finely

2 cloves garlic, crushed

2 tablespoons finely chopped fresh rosemary

1 teaspoon cumin seeds

8 baby eggplants (480g), sliced thickly

6 small yellow zucchini (540g), sliced thickly

1/2 cup (125ml) water

1/2 cup (40g) flaked parmesan cheese

Quarter capsicums; remove and discard seeds and membranes. Roast under grill or in very hot oven, skin-side up, until skin blisters and blackens. Cover capsicum with plastic or paper for 5 minutes; peel away skin and discard. Slice yellow capsicum into thin strips.
Cook pasta in large saucepan of boiling water, uncovered, until just tender; drain.
Process red capsicum, undrained tomatoes, paste and sambal until smooth.
Heat oil in wok; stir-fry onion, garlic, rosemary and seeds until onion is soft. Add eggplant and zucchini; stir-fry until zucchini is just tender.
Add pasta, tomato mixture, yellow capsicum, the water and half of the cheese; stir-fry, tossing until heated through. Serve topped with remaining cheese.

SERVES 4
Per serving 10.6g fat; 2638kJ

spiral pasta with broad beans, capsicum
and bocconcini

375g spiral pasta

2 medium red capsicums (400g)

1/3 cup (80ml) olive oil

1 small leek (200g), sliced thinly

250g asparagus, chopped coarsely

200g button mushrooms, halved

3 cloves garlic, crushed

500g frozen broad beans, thawed, peeled

2 tablespoons coarsely chopped fresh oregano

200g bocconcini, chopped coarsely

Cook pasta in large saucepan of boiling water, uncovered, until just tender; drain.

Quarter capsicums, remove and discard seeds and membranes. Roast under grill or in very hot oven, skin-side up, until skin blisters and blackens. Cover capsicum with plastic or paper for 5 minutes; peel away and discard skin. Cut capsicum into thick strips.

Heat oil in wok; stir-fry leek, asparagus, mushrooms and garlic until asparagus is just tender. Add pasta, capsicum, beans and oregano; stir-fry, tossing until hot. Remove wok from heat; toss through cheese.

SERVES 4
Per serving 27.6g fat; 2818kJ

potatoes and noodles with
chilli vegetables

Combine turmeric and potatoes in large saucepan, add water to cover; bring to a boil. Simmer, uncovered, until potatoes are tender; drain.
Rinse noodles under hot water; drain. Transfer to large bowl; separate noodles. Whisk eggs and the water in small bowl. Heat oil in wok; add egg, swirl wok so egg forms a thin omelette; cook until set. Remove from wok, roll omelette tightly; slice thinly.
Heat ghee in wok; stir-fry chilli paste until fragrant. Add onion; stir-fry until soft. Add remaining ingredients; stir-fry until cabbage is wilted. Add potato, noodles and half the omelette; stir-fry, tossing until hot. Serve with remaining omelette.
Chilli Paste Blend or process ingredients until finely chopped.

SERVES 4
Per serving 15g fat; 1739kJ

1 teaspoon ground turmeric

400g tiny new potatoes, halved

300g fresh rice noodles

2 eggs

1 tablespoon water

1 teaspoon vegetable oil

40g ghee

2 medium brown onions (300g), sliced thinly

2 small tomatoes (260g), halved, sliced thinly

2 cups (160g) bean sprouts

2 cups (160g) finely shredded chinese cabbage

2 tablespoons light soy sauce

2 tablespoons tomato sauce

chilli paste

2 teaspoons sambal oelek

4 cloves garlic, halved

4 shallots, halved

tofu with chilli
peanut sauce

vegetable oil,
for deep-frying

500g fresh firm tofu,
chopped coarsely

1 tablespoon peanut oil

2 small red capsicums
(300g), sliced thinly

150g sugar snap peas

500g spinach, trimmed

2 cups (160g) bean sprouts

2 cloves garlic, crushed

3 red thai chillies,
sliced thinly

2 teaspoons sambal oelek

$^1/_4$ cup (70g) crunchy
peanut butter

2 teaspoons palm sugar

1 tablespoon dry sherry

1 tablespoon hoisin sauce

1 tablespoon kecap manis

1 tablespoon sweet
chilli sauce

$^3/_4$ cup (180ml) water

$^1/_3$ cup (50g) unsalted
roasted peanuts

4 green onions,
chopped finely

1 tablespoon finely chopped
fresh coriander

Heat vegetable oil in wok; deep-fry tofu
until browned, drain on absorbent paper.
Heat peanut oil in clean wok; stir-fry
capsicum, peas, spinach and sprouts until
vegetables are just tender. Remove
vegetables from wok; cover to keep warm.
Add garlic and chilli to wok; stir-fry until
fragrant. Add combined sambal, peanut
butter, sugar, sherry, sauces, water and
nuts; stir until sauce comes to a boil. Add
onion, coriander and tofu; stir until hot.
Serve tofu and sauce on vegetables.

SERVES 4
Per serving 35.7g fat; 2095kJ

creamy mushrooms with
spinach and penne

500g penne

2 tablespoons olive oil

1/2 cup (70g) slivered almonds

6 green onions, chopped finely

2 cloves garlic, crushed

200g button mushrooms, halved

200g baby portobello mushrooms, halved

100g spinach, chopped coarsely

300ml cream

1 cup (80g) finely grated parmesan cheese

2 tablespoons finely shredded fresh basil

Cook pasta in large saucepan of boiling water, uncovered, until just tender; drain.
Heat 1 teaspoon of the oil in wok; stir-fry nuts until browned lightly, remove from wok.
Heat remaining oil in wok; stir-fry onion, garlic and mushrooms until mushrooms are soft and browned lightly. Add pasta, spinach, cream, cheese and basil; stir-fry, tossing until heated through. Serve topped with nuts.

SERVES 4
Per serving 59.8g fat; 4282kJ

glossary

beetroot also known as red beets or simply beets; firm, round root vegetable. Can be eaten raw or cooked.

bocconcini balls of fresh "baby" mozzarella; delicate, semi-soft, white cheese that must be kept under refrigeration, in brine, for one or two days at most.

bok choy see page 33.

breadcrumbs
packaged: fine-textured, crunchy, commercially purchased particles.
stale: one- or two-day-old bread grated, blended or processed into crumbs.

broad bean see page 32.

burghul also known as bulghur wheat; hulled, steamed wheat kernels that are dried then crushed into various-sized grains.

butter use salted or unsalted ("sweet") butter; 125g is equal to one stick butter.

capsicum also known as bell pepper or, simply, pepper. Discard seeds and membranes before use.

chickpea also known as garbanzos, channa or hummus; irregularly round sandy-coloured legume.

chinese cabbage see page 33.

choy sum see page 33.

cornflour also known as cornstarch; used as a thickening agent in cooking.

couscous a fine, grain-like cereal product, made from semolina.

eggplant also known as aubergine.

five-spice powder a fragrant blend of ground cinnamon, cloves, star anise, sichuan pepper and fennel seeds.

garam masala a blend of roasted, ground spices; can include cardamom, cinnamon, cloves, coriander, fennel and cumin.

ghee clarified butter; with the milk solids removed, this fat can be heated to a high temperature and not burn.

green bean see page 32.

hoisin sauce a thick, sweet and spicy Chinese paste made from salted fermented soy beans, onions and garlic; used as a marinade or baste.

kecap manis also spelt ketjap manis; Indonesian thick soy sauce which has sugar and spices added.

kumara Polynesian name of orange-fleshed sweet potato often confused with yam.

lemon grass a tall, clumping, lemon-smelling and -tasting, sharp-edged grass; use the white lower part of stem.

mirin a sweet Japanese low-alcohol rice wine.

mushrooms
black fungi: also known as cloud ear. Cultivated in steam rooms; cook briefly.
portobello: mature swiss browns. Large, dark-brown mushrooms with full-bodied flavour.
shiitake: also known as donko or chinese mushrooms; have unique meaty flavour. Often sold dried; soak to rehydrate before use.
shimeji: mild-flavoured, firm-textured variety resembling small oyster mushrooms but grown in clusters. Colour ranges from off-white to woody-brown.
straw: chinese mushroom with earthy flavour; usually sold canned in brine.
swiss brown: light- to dark-brown mushrooms with full-bodied flavour; also known as roman or cremini.

noodles

fresh rice: thick, wide, almost white noodles; made from rice and vegetable oil.

hokkien: fresh wheat-flour noodles resembling thick, yellow-brown spaghetti.

rice stick: dried noodle made from rice flour and water.

singapore: cryovac-packed, pre-cooked wheat noodle that is similar to hokkien noodles, but thinner.

dried wheat: dried noodles made from wheat flour, salt and water.

oil

peanut: made from ground peanuts; has very high smoke point.

sesame oil: made from roasted white sesame seeds; a flavouring rather than a cooking medium.

okra also known as bamia or lady fingers; green, ridged, oblong pod with a furry skin. Used in cooking to thicken and add flavour.

onion

green: also known as scallion or (incorrectly) shallot; an immature onion having a long, green edible stalk.

red: also known as spanish, red spanish or bermuda onion; sweet, purplish-red large onion.

spring: have crisp, narrow green-leafed tops and a small, sweet, white bulb.

plum sauce thick dipping sauce made from plums, vinegar, sugar and chilli.

pumpkin also known as squash.

raisins large, mostly seedless dried grapes.

rice vinegar made from rice (fermented), flavoured with sugar and salt. Also known as seasoned rice vinegar.

rocket see page 33.

sambal oelek also spelled ulek or olek. Paste made from chillies and vinegar.

shallot also called french shallot, golden shallot or eschalot; small, elongated and brown-skinned, it grows in clusters, and has strong onion and garlic flavour.

snake bean see page 32.

snow pea see page 32.

spinach see page 33.

squash also known as patty-pan, scallopine or summer squash.

sugar we used granulated table sugar (crystal sugar) unless otherwise specified.

brown: fine, soft granulated sugar retaining molasses.

palm: very fine sugar; also known as gula jawa, gula melaka and jaggery. Brown or black sugar can be used.

sugar snap pea see page 32.

tempeh produced by natural culture of soy beans; has a chunky, chewy texture.

tofu

firm: compressed bean curd.

fried: cubes of soft bean curd deep-fried until brown.

tomato

paste: triple-concentrated tomato puree.

sauce: also known as ketchup or catsup.

water chestnuts small brown tubers with crisp, nutty flesh.

white beans small white beans also known as butter beans or cannellini beans; available in cans.

wild rice not actually a member of the rice family; has delicious nutty flavour.

zucchini also known as courgette.

index

facts and figures 63

These conversions are approximate only, but the difference between an exact and the approximate conversion of various liquid and dry measures is minimal and will not affect your cooking results.

Measuring equipment

The difference between one country's measuring cups and another's is, at most, within a 2 or 3 teaspoon variance. (For the record, 1 Australian metric measuring cup holds approximately 250ml.) The most accurate way of measuring dry ingredients is to weigh them. For liquids, use a clear glass or plastic jug having metric markings.

Note: NZ, Canada, USA and UK all use 15ml tablespoons. Australian tablespoons measure 20ml.
All cup and spoon measurements are level.

How to measure

When using graduated measuring cups, shake dry ingredients loosely into the appropriate cup. Do not tap the cup on a bench or tightly pack the ingredients unless directed to do so. Level the top of measuring cups and measuring spoons with a knife. When measuring liquids, place a clear glass or plastic jug having metric markings on a flat surface to check accuracy at eye level.

Dry Measures		Liquid Measures		Helpful Measures	
metric	imperial	metric	imperial	metric	imperial
15g	1/2oz	30ml	1 fluid oz	3mm	1/8in
30g	1oz	60ml	2 fluid oz	6mm	1/4in
60g	2oz	100ml	3 fluid oz	1cm	1/2in
90g	3oz	125ml	4 fluid oz	2cm	3/4in
125g	4oz (1/4lb)	150ml	5 fluid oz (1/4 pint/1 gill)	2.5cm	1in
155g	5oz	190ml	6 fluid oz	6cm	21/2in
185g	6oz	250ml (1cup)	8 fluid oz	8cm	3in
220g	7oz	300ml	10 fluid oz (1/2 pint)	20cm	8in
250g	8oz (1/2lb)	500ml	16 fluid oz	23cm	9in
280g	9oz	600ml	20 fluid oz (1 pint)	25cm	10in
315g	10oz	1000ml (1litre)	13/4 pints	30cm	12in (1ft)
345g	11oz				
375g	12oz (3/4lb)				
410g	13oz	**Oven Temperatures**			
440g	14oz	These oven temperatures are only a guide.			
470g	15oz	Always check the manufacturer's manual.			
500g	16oz (1lb)				
750g	24oz (11/2lb)				
1kg	32oz (2lb)				

We use large eggs having an average weight of 60g.

Oven Temperatures

	°C (Celsius)	°F (Fahrenheit)	Gas Mark
Very slow	120	250	1
Slow	150	300	2
Moderately slow	160	325	3
Moderate	180 –190	350 – 375	4
Moderately hot	200 – 210	400 – 425	5
Hot	220 – 230	450 – 475	6
Very hot	240 – 250	500 – 525	7

at your fingertips

These elegant slipcovers store up to 10 mini books and make the books instantly accessible.

And the metric measuring cups and spoons make following our recipes a piece of cake.

Book Holder
Australia and overseas:
$A8.95 (incl. GST).

Metric Measuring Set
Australia: $6.50 (incl. GST).
New Zealand: $A8.00.
Elsewhere: $A9.95.
Prices include postage and handling.
This offer is available in all countries.

Photocopy and complete the coupon below

Mail or fax Photocopy and complete the coupon below and post to AWW Home Library Reader Offer, ACP Direct, PO Box 7036, Sydney NSW 1028, *or* fax to (02) 9267 4363.

Phone Have your credit card details ready, then, if you live in Sydney, phone 9260 0000; if you live elsewhere in Australia, phone 1800 252 515 (free call, Mon-Fri, 8.30am - 5.30pm).

Australian residents We accept the credit cards listed on the coupon, money orders and cheques.

Overseas residents We accept the credit cards listed on the coupon, drafts in $A drawn on an Australian bank, and also British, New Zealand and U.S. cheques in the currency of the country of issue.

☐ **Book holder**   ☐ **Metric measuring set**
Please indicate number(s) required.

Mr/Mrs/Ms _____

Address _____

_____

Postcode _____ Country _____

Phone: Business hours ( ) _____

I enclose my cheque/money order for $_____ payable to ACP Direct

OR: please charge $ _____ to my: ☐ Bankcard ☐ Visa

☐ Amex ☐ MasterCard ☐ Diners Club   Expiry Date ___/___

Cardholder's signature _____

Please allow up to 30 days for delivery within Australia.

Allow up to 6 weeks for overseas deliveries. Both offers expire 31/12/02.

HLMVSF02

Food editor Pamela Clark
Associate food editor Karen Hammial
Assistant food editor Kathy McGarry
Assistant recipe editor Elizabeth Hooper

HOME LIBRARY STAFF
Editor-in-chief Susan Tomnay
Editor Julie Collard
Concept design Jackie Richards
Designer Caryl Wiggins
Book sales manager Jennifer McDonald
Production manager Carol Currie

Publisher Sue Wannan
Group publisher Jill Baker
Chief executive officer John Alexander

Produced by *The Australian Women's Weekly* Home Library, Sydney.

Colour separations by
ACP Colour Graphics Pty Ltd, Sydney.
Printing by Dai Nippon Printing in Hong Kong.

Published by ACP Publishing Pty Limited,
54 Park St, Sydney; GPO Box 4088, Sydney,
NSW 1028. Ph: (02) 9282 8618
Fax: (02) 9267 9438.

awwhomelib@acp.com.au
www.awwbooks.com.au

Australia Distributed by Network Distribution Company, GPO Box 4088, Sydney, NSW 1028. Ph: (02) 9282 8777 Fax: (02) 9264 3278.

United Kingdom Distributed by Australian Consolidated Press (UK), Moulton Park Busines Centre, Red House Road, Moulton Park, Northampton, NN3 6AQ. Ph: (01604) 497 531 Fax: (01604) 497 533 acpukltd@aol.com

Canada Distributed by Whitecap Books Ltd, 351 Lynn Ave, North Vancouver, BC, V7J 2C4, Ph: (604) 980 9852.

New Zealand Distributed by Netlink Distribution Company, Level 4, 23 Hargreaves St, College Hill, Auckland 1, Ph: (9) 302 7616.

South Africa Distributed by:
PSD Promotions (Pty) Ltd, PO Box 1175, Isando 1600, SA, Ph: (011) 392 6065; and CNA Limited, Newsstand Division, PO Box 107 Johannesburg 2000. Ph: (011) 491 7500.

Vegetarian stir-fries.

Includes index.
ISBN 1 86396 246 8.

1. Vegetarian cookery.
I. Title: Australian Women's Weekly.
(Series: Australian Women's Weekly Make it Tonight mini series).

641.5636

© ACP Publishing Pty Limited 2002
ABN 18 053 273 546

Cover: Rice noodles with omelette strips and choy sum, page 44.
Stylist: Cherise Koch
Photographer: Ian Hofstetter
Back cover: Warm lentil salad, page 25.